VOCAL · GUITAR

2 0 1 5
MODERN WORSHIP HITS

Alfred

Produced by
Alfred Music
P.O. Box 10003
Van Nuys, CA 91410-0003
alfred.com

Printed in USA.

ISBN-10: 1-4706-2395-1
ISBN-13: 978-1-4706-2395-1

CONTENTS

10,000 REASONS (BLESS THE LORD)

Words and Music by
MATT REDMAN
and JONAS MYRIN

Verse 1 (Sing 1st time only):

Verse 2 (Sing 2nd time only):

Verse 3:

on that day when my strength is fail - ing, the end draws near and my time has come,___ still my soul will sing Your___ praise un - end - ing,___ ten thou - sand years and then for - ev - er - more. Bless the

Chorus:

AT THE CROSS
(LOVE RAN RED)

Words and Music by
ED CASH, JONAS MYRIN,
MATT ARMSTRONG and MATT REDMAN

Moderately slow ♩ = 73

Verse 1:

1. There's a_____ place_____ where mer - cy_____ reigns_____ and nev - er_____ dies._____ There's a_____

At the Cross (Love Ran Red) - 9 - 1

Chorus:

BROKEN VESSELS
(AMAZING GRACE)

Words and Music by
JOEL HOUSTON and JONAS MYRIN

Chorus:

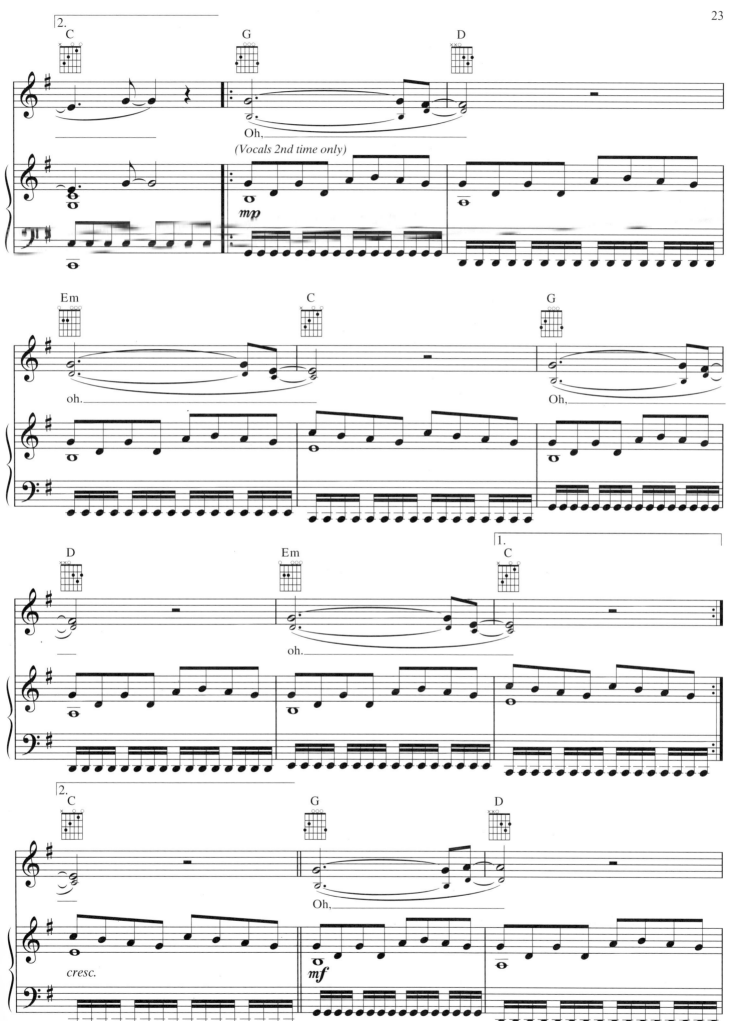

Chorus:

COME AS YOU ARE

Words and Music by
BEN GLOVER, DAVID CROWDER
and MATT MAHER

Slowly, in a passionate worship style ♩. = 45 (♪ = 135)

(with pedal)

Verse 1:

1. Come out of sad-ness from wher-ev-er you've been. Come bro-ken heart-ed, let

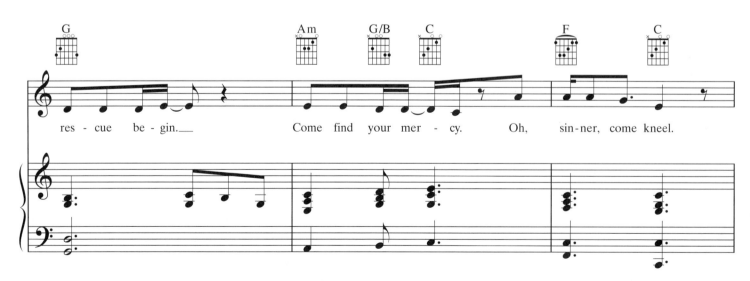

res-cue be-gin.___ Come find your mer-cy. Oh, sin-ner, come kneel.

come home,_____ you're not too_____ far. So lay down your

hurt, lay down your_ heart. Come as you are._____

2. There's

Verse 2:

hope for the hope-less and all those who've strayed. Come sit at the ta-ble,

I AM NOT ALONE

Words and Music by
AUSTIN DAVIS, BEN DAVIS,
DUSTIN SAUDER, GRANT PITTMAN,
KARI JOBE, MARTY SAMPSON
and MIA FIELDS

Verse 2:

CORNERSTONE

Words and Music by
EDWARD MOTE, ERIC LILJERO,
JONAS MYRIN and REUBEN MORGAN

Moderately slow, but majestic ♩ = 72

(with pedal)

Verse 1:

1. My hope is built on noth-ing less than Je-sus blood and right-eous-ness. I dare not trust the sweet-est frame,

45

48

FOREVER

Words and Music by
BRIAN JOHNSON, CHRISTA BLACK GIFFORD,
GABE WILSON, JENN JOHNSON,
JOEL TAYLOR and KARI JOBE

Worshipful ballad ♩ = 72

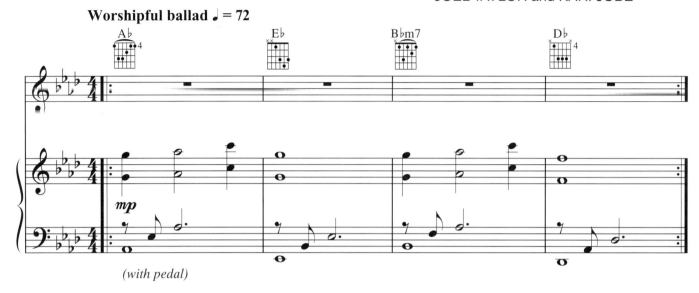

(with pedal)

Verse:

1. The moon and stars, they wept. The morn - ing sun was
2. One fi - nal breath He gave as heav - en looked a -

dead. The Sav - ior of the world was fall - en. His bod - y on the
way; the Son of God was laid in dark - ness. A bat - tle in the

*Play cue notes 2nd time.

Chorus:

Pre-Chorus:

Chorus:

IT IS WELL

Words and Music by
KRISTENE DiMARCO

It Is Well - 8 - 1

calmed and bro - ken for my re - gard. And through it

thrown in - to____ the midst of the sea. And through it

Chorus 1:

all, through it all, my eyes are on You.____ And through it all, through it all, it is well.____

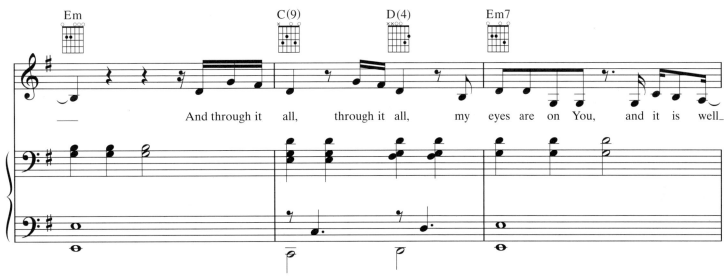

____ And through it all, through it all, my eyes are on You, and it is well____

It Is Well - 8 - 2

LORD, I NEED YOU

Words and Music by
CHRISTY NOCKELS, DANIEL CARSON,
JESSE REEVES, KRISTIAN STANFILL
and MATT MAHER

Moderate acoustic rock feel ♩ = 74

Verse 1:

Chorus:

Verse 2:

OPEN UP THE HEAVENS

Words and Music by
MEREDITH ANDREWS, JASON INGRAM,
STUART GARRARD, ANDI ROZIER
and JAMES McDONALD

Open up the Heavens - 7 - 1

Cue notes first time only

Bridge:

Show us,   show us___ Your glo - ry.   Show us,

show us___ Your pow - er.   Show us,   show us___ Your glo - ry, Lord.___

Show us,

C
E♭
show us Your glo - ry.
Show us,
show us Your pow - er.
Em
Gm
D
F
C
E♭
Show us,
show us Your glo - ry, Lord.
cresc. poco a poco
G
B♭
Oh,
oh,
oh,
C(9)
E♭(9)
We want to see You.
oh,
We want to see You.
oh.

MY HEART IS YOURS

Words and Music by
BRETT YOUNKER, DANIEL CARSON,
JASON INGRAM and KRISTIAN STANFILL

Chorus:

Interlude: (vocal ad lib.)

I just wan-na be with You.___ I just wan-na

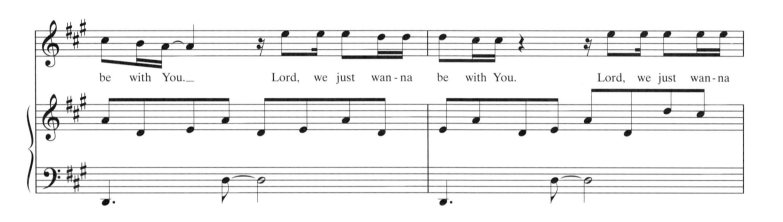

be with You.___ Lord, we just wan-na be with You. Lord, we just wan-na

be with You. Oh, wher-ev - er You are, and wher-ev - er You're

1.2. **3.**

go - ing. We just wan-na be with You. be with You. My

Chorus:

OCEANS (WHERE FEET MAY FAIL)

Words and Music by
JOEL HOUSTON, MATT CROCKER
and SALOMON LIGHTHELM

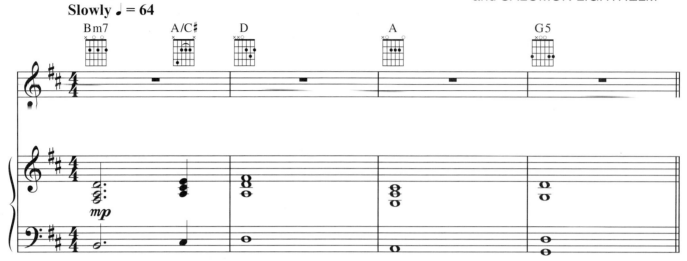

Slowly ♩ = 64

Verse:

1. You call me out up-on the wa-ters, the great un-known where feet may_ fail.
2. Your grace a-bounds in deep-est wa-ters, Your sov-'reign_ hand will be my_ guide.

And there I find You in the mys-t'ry, in o-ceans_
Where feet may fail and fear sur-rounds me, You've nev-er_

*Play cue sized notes 2nd time only.

2.
G
G
A
Yours and You are
Bm7
A/C♯
D
A
mine, oh.
f
G
Bm7
A/C♯
And You are mine, oh.
D
A
G

Bridge:

Chorus:

THIS I BELIEVE (THE CREED)

Words and Music by
BEN FIELDING and MATT CROCKER

Chorus:

Verse 2:

2. Our judge and our de-fend-er, suf-fered and cru-ci-fied. For-give-ness is in___ ___ You.

De-scend-ed in-to dark-ness, You rose in glo-ri-ous__ light, for-ev-er seat-ed___ high.__

cresc.

Chorus:

I be-lieve in God our Fath-er.__

Chorus:

Chorus:

THIS IS AMAZING GRACE

Words and Music by
JOSH FARRO, JEREMY RIDDLE
and PHIL WICKHAM

This Is Amazing Grace - 7 - 1

Chorus:

WHOM SHALL I FEAR
(GOD OF ANGEL ARMIES)

Words and Music by
CHRIS TOMLIN, ED CASH
and SCOTT CASH

Moderately slow rock ♩ = 75

On the original recording, acoustic guitars play with capo 5.

Whom Shall I Fear (God of Angel Armies) - 7 - 1